TALKS WITH THOMAS HARDY
AT MAX GATE 1920-1922

TALKS WITH THOMAS HARDY
AT MAX GATE
1920-1922

VERE H. COLLINS

DUCKWORTH

Reprinted 1978
First published 1928
Copyright © Vere H. Collins
Gerald Duckworth & Co. Ltd.
The Old Piano Factory
43 Gloucester Crescent, London NW1

ISBN 0 7156 1280 8

Printed in Great Britain by offset lithography by
Billing & Sons Ltd, Guildford, London and Worcester

INTRODUCTION

" There I put inside my breast
A moulted feather, an eagle-feather."

DURING the years 1920-1922 it fell to my great
good fortune to visit Thomas Hardy at Max
Gate, Dorchester, and to have several long conversations with him. To give to the world as
full and faithful a record as possible of what
he said at these meetings needs no apology—
even although that involves reciting in detail
what his visitor also said. The circumstances in
which my acquaintance with Hardy began
and which resulted in so notable an experience
may also, it is hoped, be thought worthy of
mention.

The first of Hardy's books that I read was
Tess of the D'Urbervilles—in 1894 (the year
in which it was published) while I was an
undergraduate at Oxford. Up to that time I
had barely known his name. In the same year
I read on its publication *Life's Little Ironies*, and
in the following year—again as soon as it appeared—*Jude the Obscure*. The reading of these
three books completed my novitiate. During
the two years that elapsed before the appearance
of his last-published novel, *The Well-Beloved*,*

* Written before *Jude the Obscure*.

v

I turned to his earlier work, and read the rest of the Wessex Novels.

For many years after that, however, I was unaware that he had written any poetry. In the August of 1904, when up in Yorkshire for a holiday, I had occasion to spend half-an-hour at Whitby waiting for a train. I went into the Public Library, took up the current number of the *Fortnightly Review*, and saw a poem by Thomas Hardy—" The Revisitation." On returning to London I bought *Wessex Poems*, and from that moment I became an enthusiastic and whole-hearted admirer of his poetry.

The subsequent publication of *Poems of the Past and Present* and the other volumes of verse which followed were to me the most noticeable literary events of the time. When rumour said that Hardy had ceased writing novels on account of adverse criticisms of *Jude the Obscure*, it seemed to me that, however much one might deplore the cause (if that were the cause), one could not feel defrauded by a result which was adding to English literature such beautiful, powerful, and original poetry. Contemporary criticism, however, remained for a long time strangely silent or cold about this poetry, apparently regarding it as the diversion of a man who was essentially a prose writer. In vain I searched for any pronouncement from the wise and the eminent treating him seriously as a poet. Lionel Johnson's *Art of Thomas Hardy*, having been published four years before *Wessex Poems*, could not, of course, have taken account of that side of his genius,* but it was a surprise and disappointment to me when, twenty years later, Mr. Lascelles Abercrombie's book, magnificent piece of criticism as it is, and though describing *The Dynasts* as " the characteristic poem of our age and one of the most momentous achievements of modern literature," gave but a meagre and frigid appreciation of the four volumes of lyrical and narrative verse which Hardy had by that date published.

In the early part of 1918 my friend Edward Thomas called on me to say good-bye before leaving for the front—where a few months later he was killed. We spent what will for ever be to me a memorable evening. Some turn in the talk led to drama and to Hardy. Thomas had seen the recent performance of *The Dynasts* in London. Suddenly, to my surprise and delight, I heard him state, in that quiet but assured way of his, that he liked Hardy's poetry more than his prose, and that it would be primarily as a poet that he would ultimately live.

Of course nothing Edward Thomas or anyone else could have said would have caused me

* Since writing this I have had my attention drawn to an article by Lionel Johnson on Hardy's poetry which appeared in the *Academy* of 12 November 1898 (reprinted in *Post Liminium*, Lane, 1911).

to cease drawing pleasure from Hardy's poetry. Nothing that others say or think is able to undermine our profoundest feelings. But none of us can remain quite impervious to the opinion of our fellow-beings. Hitherto a doubt had sometimes assailed me whether the supreme significance to me of Hardy's poems might not be due to my predilection for the particular currents underlying its philosophy and emotion, and whether my own estimate would be confirmed by those who were better qualified to assess its value as poetry. It was therefore an intense gratification to hear that my view was shared by a person in whose literary judgment I had well-nigh unbounded confidence. Henceforth I was emboldened to hold my opinion without misgivings.

In 1919 Hardy's *Collected Poems* was published. I was prompted by the occasion to re-read all his poetry. A comparison of the text with that of the original volumes disclosed numerous alterations. It was on the completion of this fascinating task, involving both a detailed scrutiny of the structure of the individual poems and a comprehensive survey from beginning to end of the whole of his poetical work (with the exception of the *Dynasts*), that there revived in me an old and ardently felt desire to see Thomas Hardy; to be in his presence—if only for a few seconds; to speak to him—or, rather, to hear him speak—if only half-a-dozen words.

For many years I had felt as Browning felt about Byron when he said that he would " at any time have gone to see a curl of his hair or one of his gloves." As far back as 1900 I had made a bicycle tour in Dorset to visit some of the places mentioned in the novels. On my route from Westerham to Dorchester I had passed Hardy's house. I dismounted, and stopped by the roadside, at the entrance to the drive, stirred by the thought that only a few yards away lived and wrote the master who seemed to me to express more beautifully and truly and poignantly than any other writer the desires and doubts, the agonies and despairs, of the heart of modern man. For some time I waited there, in the faint hope of catching a glimpse of him on his way up to or from the house. I speculated whether if he suddenly appeared I should dare to address him. But my boldness was not put to the test: darkness fell, and he did not appear. I went on to Dorchester, where I had arranged to stay a couple of nights. On the following day I rode out of the town, over the stone bridge crossing the stream in which Henchard thought of drowning himself; along the road where Fanny Robin dragged her weary limbs to lay them in Casterbridge Poorhouse; to Puddletown and Egdon Heath, and eventually to my furthest point east—the obelisk near Charborough House (the original

ix

of Welland House) where at the beginning of *Two on a Tower* Viviette first saw Swithin, and where in the last chapter " sudden joy after despair had touched an over-strained heart too smartly " and she died in his arms. That evening after getting back to Dorchester I returned to my vigil outside Max Gate. But again nothing happened; and I did not dare to walk up to the house, ring the bell, and ask to see Mr. Hardy. On the next day I had to return to London. . . .

And now again I felt, after twenty years, so strong a desire to see him, that I began to consider the question of writing to ask him whether, if I called on him at Dorchester, he would grant me a short interview. I had no excuse to urge for asking to see him except what might appear to be idle curiosity. I knew no one who could give me an introduction. I realised that to admire an author's work afforded no claim to intrude oneself on him, and that such a request might, with every justification, be refused. Nevertheless, finally, in April 1926, I wrote; I said with what delight and admiration I had been reading the *Collected Poems*— would he see me for a few minutes?

I received a reply that on 9th April he would see me for the few minutes I asked. On that date I travelled down to Dorchester from London and paid my call at the appointed hour. What I had never dared to hope would be more than a handshake and a few polite words was extended by Mr. and Mrs. Hardy's courtesy and kindness into a visit of over two hours. My first visit was succeeded by others. . . . The rest is told in the " Talks."

At having sat in the same room with Thomas Hardy and having had these long and informal conversations I have never ceased to marvel. It would be false modesty, and, moreover, a slur on that precious experience, to pretend that there must not have entered into my good fortune the happy accident that Hardy felt for me some degree of instinctive liking. But it would be correspondingly absurd not to look for some other factor which, at all events in the early stages of my relations with him, helps to explain what befell an obscure stranger without credentials who had approached by letter the greatest living English writer, then of an advanced age when a man is not disposed to take up new acquaintances. I think undoubtedly the explanation is that when I met him his poetry was still suffering from comparative neglect; that, though I did not know it at the start, he felt some disappointment and hurt at this neglect; and that I— because I felt that concerning his prose, in which he had written nothing new for eighteen years, all that was to be said had already been adequately and finely said by Lionel Johnson and Lascelles Abercrombie—was more interested in his verse—which he was still writing—and, in my first letter to him asking for an interview, as well as in my talks with him, revealed this.

When I met Hardy he was an old man of eighty. I hesitate at the word "old," so opposed is it in its ordinary associations to the vigour of intellect and the liveliness of sentiment which marked his conversation; the quickness of his thought; the versatility of his interests; the alertness in his voice, his gestures, his walk; his keenness of sight;* the extraordinary clearness and steadiness of his handwriting†—all outward signs of that vitality which produced between the ages of seventy and eighty-five four volumes of verse, ‡ throughout which, whether we regard the intellectual or emotional force or the technique, it is impossible to detect the slightest mark of any falling-off from his earliest work.

In his manner Hardy was quiet—though genial—and unassuming. He was very ready to respond to any question, and to follow

* See e.g. page 82.

† See page 59, and cf. page 73. The writing of the notes on the margins of Mr. Hedgcock's book might have been that of a young man of twenty.

‡ Subsequent to the publication in 1910 of *Time's Laughing-stocks and Other Verses*, there appeared in 1914 *Satires of Circumstance*, in 1917 *Moments of Vision*, in 1922 *Late Lyrics and Earlier*, in 1925 *Human Shows, Far Fantasies*.

up any subject that was introduced. (I noticed that he seemed to prefer that the thread of conversation should be directed by me.) The expression of his thought flowed easily and informally—often as of a person thinking aloud; sometimes in a half-questioning tone as if inviting rather than demanding assent. Literature was our chief topic of conversation, but he showed very little disposition to enter into literary theories and principles.* The references he made to his own work were always modest, and very practical†—the attitude of a craftsman towards a trade, with no tendency to regard the writing of books as an elevated pursuit superior to that of the common man—though, having chosen the career of letters, he made no pretence of not being concerned by the fortunes that befell his work. His references to contemporary writers were generously free from any note of jealousy or malice; he was specially interested in the work of the younger poets.

In the last poem of *Moments of Vision* (" Afterwards "), where Hardy imagines how, after he is dead, those who had known him may speak of him, he describes their remembrance

* Cf. the opinion expressed in his Introduction to the *Selected Poems of William Barnes* (Oxford University Press, 1908): " The history of criticism is mainly the history of error."

† See e.g. his remarks on the origin of *The Dynasts*, page 83.

of him as of one who was interested to notice the sights and sounds of both the great and the small things of external nature—the starry heavens, the wind, the flight of a moth, the crawl of a hedgehog. This side of him it was not my lot to have opportunities of observing. Towards the end of *Time's Laughingstocks* there is another poem in which he describes himself. When my memory goes back to those visits to Max Gate and my talks there with Thomas Hardy and his wife, and I try to fix that final impression which crystallizes from the words, the appearance, the voice, and a dozen other things in a person, but which often seems unconnected with any definite point one has been conscious of, it is this poem, *A Poet*, that comes to my mind and seems to sum up the essential Hardy—the man to whom life stood for more than art, and the love of man and woman for more than success and fame.

CONTENTS

Persons :

Mr. Thomas Hardy	H
Mrs. Thomas Hardy	Mrs. H
Mr. Collins	C

I

9 *April* 1920. *The drawing-room at Max Gate,
Dorchester, into which* C *has just been shown.*

Mrs. H [*after shaking hands with him*]: I will go
and tell my husband you are here. I don't think
he heard the bell ring. [*She leaves the room.*]

C *looks round. On the left of the fireplace he
notices below a photograph of* Mrs. H *a photograph of Galsworthy, with an autograph quotation
from one of the latter's stories, giving a definition
of Optimism and Pessimism.* While he is reading
this* Mrs. H *re-enters, with her husband.* H *and* C
shake hands.

H *is about five feet five in height. He is dressed
in an old, yellowish brown tweed suit. Aged* 79,
he might easily be taken for not older than about
65. *His carriage is erect; his movements brisk;
eyes bright and steady; utterance clear and strong;
hearing perfect. He inclines to spareness, but
for an old man of that habit he is noticeably not
very thin. His complexion is healthy, and neither
ruddy nor pale. He has a quiet, easy manner: com-
posed, unassertive, but alert. His face is deeply
lined, but the expression is not melancholy.*

Mrs. H *serves tea from a large round table,
near which all three sit informally.* Mrs. H *is*

* See page 62.

I

on C's right. H *on his left.* H *sits upright in a straight-backed, armless chair.*

C: I have been talking to Mrs. Hardy of the days when she used to come to see one of my colleagues about those books she wrote for the Oxford Press.

H: What is the relation of Raleigh to the Oxford University Press?

C: He is one of the Delegates—what would be Directors in an ordinary commercial firm, but they give their services without payment.

H: Do you often go to Oxford?

C: Fairly often. I was sorry I was not able to get there for the performance of *The Dynasts*. I saw it when it was done some years ago in London. May I know which of the two performances you preferred?

H: Of course neither was complete. There were only about thirty scenes out of 150. It was really a misnomer to call it *The Dynasts*. I suppose, however, they had to. On the whole I preferred the Oxford performance, because it was done by young men. Moreover, in London the effect was too much as if the whole thing occurred indoors. Even the battles looked as if they were under architraves. I wrote to the people at Oxford about this, and it was altered. I thought the Nelson scene was rather too noisy.

C: In London I thought that the whole performance erred very much on that side. Ainley was too loud and declamatory in reading the stage directions, which it seemed to me ought to have been read very quietly. The actors also were often very noisy—so that, what with Ainley's bellowing, and the aides-de-camp rushing up shouting to Wellington and Napoleon, the whole effect lost both dignity and verisimilitude.

H: I see no reason why the reader of the stage directions should not be invisible.

C: I heard of the enthusiastic demonstration that was given you at Oxford, and how the undergraduates called for " Author " after you had left.

H: I assure you it was from no discourtesy that I left at the end of the performance. I had an appointment with Raleigh. . . .

C: I see that *Tess* is being shown on the films.

H: I was present at a rehearsal of it in the United States.

C: Are others of the novels to be done too?

H: I don't know. I leave all that to Macmillan. My experience of seeing film plays has been unfortunate. There always seem to be motor-cars rushing over cliffs and people jumping out of windows. What effect do you think the cinematograph will have on the sale of books?

C: I should have thought that it would appeal to a public that only read sensational novels.

H: I was surprised that people cared for *Tess* on the film, for it always seems to be mainly young people who go to see the cinematograph. . . .

C: I have been collating your *Collected Poems*, Mr. Hardy, with the original editions, and have been very much interested to see what a large number of alterations you have made.

H: I made the corrections as I went along. There are a considerable number of misprints in the Collected Edition. Macmillan has issued an errata slip. Had your copy one?

C: No, but I bought the book when it first came out.

H: I will get a copy of the slip for you. [*He leaves the room.*]

Mrs. H: Are you stopping at Dorchester?

C: No; I am returning to London this evening. . . . Will you tell me quite frankly if I had better go now? I do not want to take up too much of Mr. Hardy's time. It was very good of him to see me at all.

Mrs. H: I am sure he is interested.

H [*returning with an errata slip which he hands to* C]: That will save you having to buy a revised edition. I cannot understand how mistakes occur in a printed book when a proof has been corrected properly.

4

C: Sometimes a word or line drops out when the formes are being moved and the printer resets carelessly without referring to the proof.

H: I remember Tennyson being very much annoyed because one of his poems was printed with " hairy does " instead of " aery does." On another occasion " mad phases " became " mud phrases."

C: I am sorry that there is not an India paper edition of the *Collected Poems*.

H: I will speak to Macmillan about it.

C: Do you know Edward Thomas's poetry?

H: I read one volume. I liked it.

C: You haven't read his second volume?

H: No. I saw that it had been published.

C: May I have the pleasure of sending you a copy?

H: Thank you, but we are crowded out for room for books. I will get it from the Times Book Club. I might buy a book like that—but I should read it first. I wonder how it was I never met him. He was often about here.

C: Yes, he was a great walker.

H: What was he like in appearance?

C: He was tall——

H: Tall?

C: Over six feet; slim, well built, with a well-shaped head. He was handsome, but his face was rather emaciated, with a melancholy expression.

H: It was very sad his being killed.

C: It was remarkable that he did not start writing poetry until he was nearly forty.

H: If he had lived, perhaps he would have had to go back to journalism and prose writing.

C: His death of course helped to draw attention to his poetry, as in a greater degree did Rupert Brooke's to his.

H: He was a friend of de la Mare, was he not?

C: Yes, and of many of the younger poets— Davies, Drinkwater, Freeman.

H: There is a lot of good work being done.

C: And the public is reading poetry more to-day than it has done for many years.

H: No doubt that is a result of the war.

C: In the schools quite considerable attention is now being paid to modern and even contemporary poetry. *Poems of To-day* has run into nearly twenty editions in a few years.

H: *Poems of To-day?*

C: The anthology of modern poetry published by the English Association.

H: Oh yes—I remember.

C: I am sorry it does not contain any of your poems.* I heard they wanted some.

H: They never asked me. I myself am a mem-

* Several of Hardy's poems were included in the Second Series of *Poems of To-day* (1922).

ber of the English Association. Perhaps they asked my publisher without offering a fee. My publisher thinks that there ought to be some small charge. Kipling charges. So many people ask, that if one gave leave all round the whole of one's poems would be read without any of the original volumes being bought.

C: I hear that Squire is doing an anthology of modern poetry.*

H: Squire is a very good man. I have not seen him lately. How is the *London Mercury* doing?

C: Very well, I believe. I am told that 10,000 of the first number were sold. . . .

C: Do you know the poetry of Squire's assistant editor Shanks?

H: I don't think I do.

Mrs. H: We read his *Queen of China*.

H: Oh yes, I remember. It is not a title that would naturally interest one. . . . Why does not Quiller-Couch continue the *Oxford Book of English Verse* to 1900? " To 1900 " would make a very telling title.

C: Of course there is his *Oxford Book of Victorian Verse*.

H: Many people cannot afford or are not willing to buy two anthologies of English poetry. I think I suggested this to Quiller-Couch.

Selections from Modern Poets (Martin Secker, 1921)

7

C: I will tell Mr. Milford what you have said. . . .

H: I seldom read novels now, but I understand that to-day they no longer have plots.

C: Many of them certainly consist of a great deal of psychology based on very little incident.

H: Perhaps the cinematograph will take the place of fiction, and novels will die out, leaving only poetry. . . .

Mrs. H: You live in the Hampstead Garden Suburb: are there many literary people there?

C: I don't know if any of the bigger lights are there. Rebecca West used to live there but she left. Have you read her last novel, *The Return of the Soldier?*

Mrs. H: Yes. I thought it well done, though the latter part tended to develop into a mere tract on Freudism. The last sentence was good. . . . [*To* H] Mr. Collins is going back to London this evening.

H: That will be very tiring. I have never known any of our visitors do the return journey in one day. I used to myself at one time, and I may have to be doing so again soon.

C: I find a journey in a train quite a rest.

H: I do not mind it, though I no longer feel as I did when I was a young man travelling abroad and thought it quite dull to sleep two consecutive nights at the same place.

C: I used to feel like that too when I was

8

younger, in my bicycling days. Fifteen years ago I made a bicycle tour in Wessex, visiting some of the places mentioned in your novels, with the help of that book of Windle's, illustrated by New.

H: The best book about that now is one done by a man called Hermann Lea, published by Macmillan. I say nothing about its literary quality: it does not attempt to do anything but be a mere guide; but it is very full and accurate. There are only three mistakes in about a hundred and fifty places identified.

C: Mr. Hardy, I hope I am not taking up too much of your time.

H: Stay as long as you like. Do not think of us, but only of your train.

C: Thank you very much.

H: What train are you thinking of catching?

C [*looking at his watch*]: The next one is at half-past seven. I have to go back to the King's Arms to get a parcel I left there. I heard that a bust of yours was to be had in the town, and after lunching at the inn I found out from the waiter where the shop was it was sold at, and bought one.

H: It was made by a Poole firm.

C: I heard at the shop that there were very few left, and that the firm which made them had come to an end.

H: I hope it was not I that ruined them.

C: Has a reproduction been made of the bust done by Thornycroft?

H: I don't think so.

C: The waiter at the King's Arms was very amusing. When he heard I wanted to buy a bust of you, he said: " I had the honour of waiting on Mr. Hardy last night. He was dining here with one of the visitors at the hotel. Mr. Hardy's host had a friend who also dined with the party. During dinner this gentleman said, ' Dorchester is a very small place to be the county town of Dorsetshire. I walked round it in half an hour.' I could not help smiling at Mr. Hardy's reply. He turned to the gentleman and said, very quietly: ' And what did you see in the half-hour? ' "

H: I know that waiter. He is quite a nice and intelligent chap. It is strange what waiters hear. The other day there was a notice in one of the newspapers that I was ill. The fact was that I had been indoors for a couple of days with a cold, but I was not ill. [*To* Mrs. H] I wonder whether the butler at ——, like the waiter at the King's Arms, finding he had opportunities of picking up information, is a correspondent for that paper. . . . [*To* C] There was also a statement in the gossip column of a lady's paper saying that I had been seen lunching with the manager of the Palladium, and that no doubt I was contemplating writing a play for him.

Perhaps in that case someone had been mistaken for me. . . . Do you think that the classes who are now better off spend money on books?

C: Not, of course, the majority, but I think a fair number. There has been a considerable increase in the number of copies of the "World's Classics" sold during the last few years, though the sale of the more expensive series of Standard Authors and Oxford Poets has gone down. There is bound to be an increase of an intelligent reading public as long as there is increased expenditure on education every year, and a larger proportion of the population undergoing secondary education.

H: I am glad to hear that. By all means let us give them money as long as it does not threaten to injure literature.

During a pause in the conversation C *notices that* H, *who has hitherto sat erect during the whole of the interview, is leaning back, with his head slightly drooping forward and the lines of his face relaxed, for the first time showing signs of fatigue.* C *rises to say good-bye to* Mrs. H. *As he does so he notices a bunch of rhododendrons in a bowl.*

C: Were these grown out in the open?

Mrs. H: They came from Lady Ilchester. [*Pointing to a framed drawing on the wall*] That is a picture of the garden.

H: They could hardly have flowered in the open so early. It has been a wonderfully mild winter, though. [*Pointing to another vase*] The blackthorn is out profusely.

C: Even in my garden at Hampstead, which has a clay soil and is in an exposed situation, there is a Gloire de Dijon rose in bud.

[C *shakes hands with* Mrs. H. H *conducts him into the hall.*]

Mr. Hardy, I will not again thank you for letting me see you. I will only say that to-day one of the chief desires of my life has been accomplished. Fifteen years ago, when on a bicycle tour in Wessex, I stopped outside Max Gate; I did not dare to go in; but I hoped that some day I might meet you. There is one other thing I should like to add, if I am not venturing on too personal a strain—that I read and re-read your poetry not only with interest and admiration, but often for the consolation that beautiful poetry brings.

H: Sometimes when one is sad it consoles one to read a sad poem.

C: When one reads poetry like yours it makes one think to oneself " What is the importance of one's own little troubles, when a master mind and a master heart has been through all that? " I hope you don't mind my having said that.

H: No, no.

12

C *puts on his hat and coat.*

H: You are sure you know the way to the station?

C: Oh yes. [*He shakes hands and goes.*]

II

27 *December* 1920. Mrs. H *and* C *in the drawing-room at Max Gate. Enter* H *from a walk, with his dog.* H *and his visitor shake hands, and sit down.* Mrs. H *serves tea. She,* H *and* C *are seated as on the previous visit.*

The dog jumps up at C *and barks.* H *orders him to lie down.*

C: I've not seen your dog before, but I have been hearing all about him, and how he made friends with Barrie, but snapped at Mrs. Granville Barker.

The dog takes a log of wood from the grate, and carries it to the hearth-rug, where he lies down gnawing it.

Mrs. H: He always does that to impress strangers.

C *asks* H *to accept a copy of the* Oxford Almanac *for* 1921 *which he has brought with him.* H *examines it with interest, asks who painted the original, and thanks* C *for it.* C *says he would like to get it framed for him.*

H: I will not trouble you to do that. I will fasten it up in my study with drawing-pins.

C: We are all very much interested in London at hearing about your local star, Miss Bugler. I am looking forward to seeing her at

14

the Guildhall School of Music next month. I suppose there will be some seats open to the general public.

H: There are sure to be. The Dorset Men reserve a certain number, and all the rest are sold to the public. They have hired the Guildhall School of Music as being larger than the Cripplegate Institute which they generally have. Do you know what size the room is, and what the hearing is like?

C: I am sorry I cannot tell you. I have never been in it.

H: They reckon on having to take about £200 to pay expenses.

C: As much as that?

H: Yes, it seems a lot. But there's the hire of the room, the return fares of about twenty persons, and their hotel expenses.

C: I should not think there will be any difficulty in getting that this year. So much notice has been given to Miss Bugler in the newspapers.

H: The truth is that the *Daily Mail* man came down here and fell in love with her.

Mrs. H: I think she will do very well—as long as she is not nervous.

H: Yes. She is exactly the physical type I had in mind when I imagined Eustacia Vye—tall and dark. I told her that she would have a much better time if she did not go on the stage as a professional, but acted now and then as an amateur. . . . Are you a musician, Mr. Collins?

C: I am sorry I am not.

H [*handing him a book of songs containing poems by Thomas Hardy ("When I set out for Lyonnesse"), de la Mare, and Ledwidge, set to music by Boyer*]: This has just been sent to me.

Mrs. H: We had the mummers here on Friday. They acted very well. Everything was done in the old style. It was a very pleasant Christmas Eve, [*to* H] was it not?

H: Yes, very. [*To* C] How is the book trade in London?

C: Fair, considering everything, but I fear that all round there is rather a slump in trade—due partly to the middle classes being poor, partly to a general feeling of uncertainty on account of the demands of labour.

H: You do not publish novels, do you?

C: No, except reprints of the classics in series like the "World's Classics."

H: Oh yes, of course, you took over the "World's Classics" from Grant Richards. . . . Some people talk of novels as if they were the only books. . . . Do you publish any of Trollope's novels?

C: Yes; we are issuing him in the "World's Classics."

H: I like Trollope. You know, at one time it

was thought he was going to be recognized as the greatest of the early Victorian novelists. Dickens was said to be too much of a caricaturist; Thackeray too much of a satirist. Trollope was put forward as the happy mean.

C: When I saw you last you said that you did not read many novels now. I was wondering the other day whether you knew Couperus's work.

H: No.

C: I have only recently for the first time been reading some of his books. They are very fine, I think. He is fortunate in being very well translated by Texeira de Mattos.

H: Is he the translator of that other man whom we have been hearing about?

C: Hamsun?

H: Yes.

C: I forget who has translated him. Not de Mattos.

Mrs. H: What other authors has de Mattos translated?

C: There's Maeterlinck and Fabre; I forget what others.

Mrs. H: I like Mrs. Garnett's translations. I have been reading some of Tchehov's stories translated by her. They are very good.

H: Is that the wife of Edward Garnett?

C: Yes.

H: The son of Richard Garnett?

C: Yes.

H: I had some correspondence with him once. He did not believe in Art. His theory was that to write a novel all one had to do was to go to a farmhouse and just describe what happened there during the day. I pointed out to him that if one wanted to make people read a book one must have something special to interest them with. I don't know if I ended by convincing him. Some of the younger men applied Garnett's idea to poetry: Siegfried Sassoon, for example. Some of his poems are quite good, though.

C: Have you read the poems of that friend of his, Owen?

H: Owen?

C: He was killed in the war. A book of his poems has just been published to which Sassoon has written an introduction.

H: Owen—oh, yes. The book was sent to me as a Christmas present. [*To* Mrs. H] I have marked some of the poems for you to read. Sassoon is a very good friend to people. I hope the book will sell well. . . . How is it that such a number of poets have gone to live at Oxford?

C: I think it started with Masefield going there. He was much lionized. Perhaps the others did not want to be left out in the cold.

H: Perhaps they thought they would get degrees. There's Yeats and Graves—and I heard Nichols was going there.

18

C: I had not heard that. But he will be leaving England now to take up his new appointment.

H: What is that?

C: He has been appointed Professor of English Literature in Japan.

H: Nichols is a good chap. He has been here. He was passing on his bicycle. I enjoyed his visit. He is very amusing and outspoken. . . . But what on earth made Yeats go to Oxford?

Mrs. H: Perhaps he is trying to convert the Oxford people to Sinn Fein.

H: Sinn Fein. Yeats is not a Sinn Feiner!

Mrs. H: He says he is. I heard that the other day he excused himself from attending a public dinner on the grounds that it would upset his friends to hear he had been present where the King's health was drunk.

H: I don't suppose he believes in Sinn Fein. I don't suppose he knows what he believes. . . .

C: Mr. Hardy, you remember I wrote to tell you that I was classifying your poems. I have now finished the classification. I don't know if it seems to you rather ridiculous to apply arithmetical tables to poetry. The other day, however, Bridges said to a friend of mine, " If you even read through a man's poems to find out how often he uses the letter z you will end by making some real discoveries about his poetry."

H: I suppose he was referring to the spelling of words like " recognize."

C: Bridges is, of course, very much interested in pronunciation and spelling, and that may have caused him to use the illustration; but I took him to mean something more general— that a thorough detailed study of a poet, from almost any point of view, would lead to familiarity with and a grasp of his methods or ideas which would repay the labour.

H: Wordsworth, you know, tried to arrange his poems into classes, but it was not successful.

C: I did not know that. Would you care to look at my results?

H: Let me see what headings you group them under.

C *produces his tables and lists, and explains briefly the principles of the classification.*

H [*looking at the table of general classification*]: I see there are most poems on " Love and Marriage." More than on " Death "—which I am told I am always bringing in. . . . [C *turns over the pages to the table sub-classifying the Love poems.*] Which comes first here? Oh—" Ill-mating and Disharmony "! [*Amused*] . . . Ah, the " Unclassified " poems!

C: But there are not many—only twenty-two out of 510.

H: That is the total number, is it?

C [*turning over to the sub-classification of the*

'*Philosophical Poems*']: "Philosophical" is rather a vague word, but I could not think of a better term under which to bring a number of poems on metaphysical and abstract themes which did not fall into the other categories.

H: Yes.

C: There are a few poems—very few: only about a dozen in all the five volumes—in which there are allusions that are obscure to me. I wonder if you would be so good as to let me ask you about them.

H: Certainly. I am very anxious not to be obscure. It is not fair to one's readers. After all, Spencer was right in saying that the energy devoted to finding out the meaning of what one reads is spent at the cost of what might have been given to appreciating it. Some of the younger poets are too obscure.

C: And some of the Victorian writers too— Meredith for example.

H: Yes, that is why his poetry has never been read much. And Doughty—*Mansoul!* Do you know it?

C: I was trying to read it the other day, but it was beyond me.

H: He often avoids Possessives —but he is not consistent. No doubt his writing is very much packed, and perhaps if one mastered his way of expressing himself one would find that it is only a trick.

C: Like Browning and Carlyle, whom one found difficult at first: but when one had got familiar with their tricks their thought was seen to be very simple. In Meredith's poetry the thought itself is obscure—and so, too, is Abercrombie's, though he is quite clear and simple in his prose.

H: What has happened to him? I heard he was very ill and in a bad way.

C: I had not heard that. Doughty is very ill, I believe.

H: He is having his portrait painted in his doctor's robe, and I lent him mine, as it was not worth his while buying one: they are so dear now—about £40, I am told. At Cambridge I hired one. At Oxford they were more hospitable: they lent me one; indeed, they made it clear from the beginning that it would not be necessary for me to buy one. . . .

C [*taking from his pocket a copy of the* Collected Poems, *and a note-book containing the required references*]: Well, Mr. Hardy, as you are so kind, may I now go through the few points in the poems of which I should be grateful for your elucidation?

H *draws his chair nearer to* C, *and reads through each poem in question as* C *turns it up.*

(*Wessex Poems*)
" Postponement "

C: I am not clear what is the human application of the last stanza—" Ah, had I been . . . born to an evergreen nesting tree."

H: You see, earlier in the poem the young man is described as not being able to marry for want of money; and the woman as not waiting, but marrying someone else.

C: I understand that. The " being born to an evergreen tree " means, then, simply and solely having money?

H: Yes.

" She, To Him "

C: I do not quite follow the idea in the last stanza. If what the man stood for, to the woman, meant so much that it is her " whole life," how can he be to her a mere " thought," like his thought of her—which is almost contemptuous and, we are told, " thin "?

H *reads the poem and proceeds to explain it. But either he fails to see* C's *difficulty, or* C *to grasp* H's *point.*

H: I think you will be able to work it out.

(*Time's Laughing-stocks*)
" The Dawn after the Dance "

C: What is " that which makes man's love the lighter and the woman's burn no brighter "?

H: I suppose when they got intimate. [*He re-reads the poem.*] I think perhaps I originally wrote " *the* brighter."

" Aberdeen "

C: Who is the " Queen "?

H: Knowledge. That might apply to any University town—though, of course, not the granite.

" Self-Unconscious "

C: In the last stanza but two, why and how " should he have been shown " as he was? What difference would it have made?

H: If he had realized then, when young, what he was, he would have acted differently. That is the tragedy of youth: when we know, it's too late to alter things.

" God's Funeral "

C: In the last stanza but one, does each mourner shake his head to mean " yes " or " no " ?

H: " No."

C: So there were three sets of people—those who thought God was dead; those who thought that a false God was dead, but that the true one still lived; and those who thought that a new and purer God was still to make himself known to man?

H: Yes.

(*Moments of Vision*)
" At Mayfair Lodgings "

C: Why, and how, " need not the tragedy have come due "? Because she would have married him, and there would not now have been the tragedy of her dying apart from him?

H: Yes.

" On a Heath "

C: Who or what is it that is referred to in the last stanza?

H: There is a third person.

C: " Another looming," " one still blooming," " a shade entombing "—are not there three different things?

H: No, only one.

" The Interloper "

C: What is " that under which best lives corrode "?

H: Madness.

C: In each case?

H: Yes. I knew the family.

Mrs. H: I always thought the poem was obscure.

H [*reads it*]: Certainly it is not clear. No one could possibly guess.

C: I asked several people, and they were all puzzled. One of my colleagues, Mr. Williams —himself a poet—suggested that it was no definite thing, but a sort of undermining rot which destroys everything.

H: That was a remarkably good guess. He got as near it as one possibly could. [*He reads the poem again, over* C's *shoulder.*] Write down " Insanity"; that is a better word than " Madness." I wonder how I could make it clear.

C: Could you add a motto, as you sometimes do—say from the Bible?

H: That is a good idea. But I fear the Bible will not do. They did not believe in madness as we understand it.

25

Mrs. H: It was always "being possessed of devils."

C: Something from classical Latin or Greek?

Mrs. H: Was there not a proverb—about the gods sending people mad?

C: "Quem deus vult perdere prius dementat." Is not that rather insolent pride—the ὕβρις of the Greeks? I suppose madness as we understand it was represented by the Furies.

H: I must do something to make it clear. "I rose and went to Rou'tor Town"

C: What is "the evil wrought at Rou'tor Town"?

H. Slander, or something of that sort. . . . [*Turning over the pages of* Collected Poems, *and pointing to* "*Near Lanivet*"] This is a poem which is often neglected. [*Turning over some more pages, and pointing to* "*At the Word Farewell*"]: This is quite a good poem too. But of course there are plenty of love poems to choose from. . . . Do you think the price of books is likely to go down?

C: I fear not for some time, and probably never back to the old prices.

H: It's a great pity. It is to the interest of authors that a large number of copies should be sold at a low price, and often of the publisher that a comparatively small number should be sold at a higher price. That seems to be the only point on which the interests of publishers and

26

authors clash. . . . Do you know how the literary papers are selling?

C: I don't suppose any of them at any time are very remunerative. I am hoping that the *Athenæum* will do well under its new editorship.

H: I thought it was rather a pity they did not change its name. But Middleton Murry is a clever chap. Who else writes for it?

C: His wife, Katharine Mansfield, does a good deal.

H: Is that " K.M."?

C: Yes.

H: I heard that his wife had been in the South of France for some time very ill, and that Middleton Murry has gone over this Christmas to see her.

C: I noticed that the scene of one or two of her sketches has been laid in the South of France.

H: That would account for it.

C: She has just published a volume of short stories.

Mrs. H: I saw a review of it—*Bliss.*

H: I have not read any short stories for a long time. Are they good?

C: I have not seen the book yet, but some of the stories appeared in the *Athenæum*, where I read them, and I thought them very good.

H: I must read the book.

C: May I know where the original drawings of the illustrations in *Wessex Poems* are?

H: I gave them to Birmingham University.

C: And the MS. as well?

H: Yes.

C: Are the other volumes of poetry there too?

H: Cambridge has one, and *Jude the Obscure*; and Oxford has one.

Mrs. H: Two, I think. *Moments of Vision* we have kept.

C: I don't know if you are interested in the prices that early editions of your books fetch.

H: Oh yes.

C: I can't as a rule afford to indulge in first editions, but I was very anxious to have a first edition of *Wessex Poems* on account of the larger sized illustrations. I was able to get a copy through Blackwell of Oxford for 18s. 6d. That, I thought, was a very good bargain.

H: I certainly think you can consider it was.

C: A short time ago I had occasion to advertise for a friend in the *Publishers' Circular* for any early editions of your books, and I have brought with me offers I received from some booksellers which I thought you might be interested to see. [C *reads out the items—mostly second editions, at prices varying from* 30s. *to* £4 4s. H *is much interested, and gives some bibliographical details of the volumes.*]

Mrs. H [*referring to the price quoted for a second edition of* A Pair of Blue Eyes]: We have not a first edition of that.

28

H: When I corrected *A Pair of Blue Eyes* for a second edition I used my own and last copy, and when the printer returned this, with the proofs of the new edition, I tore it up.

Mrs. H: A friend of ours is very anxious to obtain a copy of it, and would go up to £30.

C: I noticed that in one of the volumes of short stories the names of the separate tales were not given on the respective right-hand pages, but only the volume's title as the heading on both pages.

H: Is that so? I must have passed it in proof. I will go and look. [*Gets up and moves towards the door.*]

C: Might I see your study?

H [*hesitatingly and edging out of the room*]: It is very untidy.

Mrs. H [*catching C's eye and smiling*]: He would feel he had to tidy it up first.

While H *is upstairs* Mrs. H *shows* C *some first editions. One of them is a two-volume edition of* The Hand of Ethelberta *with drawings by Du Maurier. Another is* Moments of Vision *inscribed " The First Copy | Of the First Edition | To the First of Women | Florence Hardy."*

H [*returning with the Mellstock edition of* Life's Little Ironies *and* Wessex Tales]: I am glad to say they are all right.

C: It must be *A Group of Noble Dames* then.

H [*to* Mrs. H]: Will you get it? [Mrs. H *leaves the room.*] It is a nice edition. The printing and paper are good. [*Mrs. H. returns with* A Group of Noble Dames *which she hands to him.*] Ah, yes, it is as you say. I wonder if there was any reason. [*He turns to the Contents.*]

C: The titles are long, but " First Dame's Tale," etc., could have been left out.

H: And the rest could have been abbreviated: " Barbara "—omitting " of the House of Grebe." I don't know how I passed it.

C: Was the title of *The Dynasts* settled from the beginning when you first started writing it?

H: I forget when I chose it. It must have been at a fairly early stage, for as you know it was published in three consecutive parts.

C: Do you pronounce the " y " long or short?

H: I think I got it from the " Magnificat " —the Greek version. The Greek " u " is short. ... I have thought of reprinting the lyrics from it—say in small type—at the end of the *Collected Poems.* Two or three of them—for example " Trafalgar " and " My Love's Gone a-fighting "—are as good as anything in the *Collected Poems.*

C: Or you could reprint them in a sixth volume of poems. That would enable your readers to possess a fresh volume sooner. You have written quite a considerable number of

30

poems since *Moments of Vision* was published, and some of them, I think, are as fine as anything you have ever written. I have in mind especially " Going and Staying " and " Mellstock Cross at the Year's End."

H: I shall probably alter the title of " Mellstock Cross." I have used it elsewhere.

C: The poem appeared in the *Fortnightly* a year ago, did it not?

H: Yes, they have asked me for another poem. But editors do not understand that one cannot always lay one's hand on a poem that is suitable for the occasion. It is better really to wait until one has written enough to publish for the first time in book form.

C: But all of us are impatient for your work. We do not want to have to wait.

H: If I reprinted the lyrics from *The Dynasts* would not people feel that they had been taken in—having to pay a second time for what they already had?

C: I am sure, Mr. Hardy, they would not feel that.

Mrs. H: Even if they possessed *The Dynasts* they might be glad to have the lyrical poems from it brought together, so as to be saved having to search them out. . . .

C: Do you like Max Beerbohm's work?

H: I do.

C: Have you ever met him?

H: No, but I have sat opposite him at a dinner. He has not at all a humorous face, I thought, but rather a melancholy expression.

C: I have not met him for many years. I was at Charterhouse with him.

H: What was he like then? Did he draw?

C: He used to do caricatures of the masters and boys. He drew a very unflattering caricature of me, which I am sorry to say I tore up.

H: That was a pity. Was he thought clever?

C: He was only half-way up the school when he left; he got a Third Class in Classical Moderations at Oxford, and went down without taking his degree. He was the only boy at Charterhouse in my time who was known never to have changed into football clothes, besides his one and inseparable companion who was lame. He was thought to be eccentric, but was not regarded as offensive, in spite of being rather a dandy—always dressed in the latest London fashion, and with his hair parted in the middle and plastered down flat. Contrary to the usual idea of the English Public School, Charterhouse, though the main interest was games, was very tolerant to unconventional boys. Of course they did not enjoy popularity, but they were left alone unless they were aggressive.

H: He lives in Italy, I understand. It must be very awkward for him, but I suppose he does not remain there all the time.

C: Have you read his last book?

H: No, but I have read some of his books.

C: *A Christmas Garland?*

H: Yes. . . . He sent me a caricature he did of me. [Mrs. H *goes to a drawer and hands* C *two drawings. One is a reduced reproduction of the well-known cartoon of—" Mr. Thomas Hardy composing a lyric." The other is an original cartoon of* H.] I wrote and asked him whether the original of his published cartoon was for sale. He replied that he had disposed of it, and had not even a copy by him, but he sent me this, which he said was his best recollection of it.

Mrs. H: I suppose we ought to get it framed. The figure is turned in the opposite direction to the figure in the published one, and it is not so good: it has a look of Bernard Shaw. And he has added a moon. That is an improvement.

C: And very appropriate too. [*To* H] The moon comes so often into your poems.

H: I suppose it docs.

C *rises to go. He says good-bye to* Mrs. H. H *accompanies him to the hall, lights a lantern, and conducts him along the drive to the gate.*

C: As a mountaineer, Mr. Hardy, I was interested to notice that you have two poems on mountains—one, on the death of Leslie Stephen, about the Shreckhorn; and one about the Matterhorn. Have you done much climbing?

33

H: I never went in for climbing. The highest point I ascended was the Riffel.

C: And I have noticed that, with the exception of the poem on Aberdeen, there is no reference to Scotland.

H: That was the only time I ever went to Scotland. It was so expensive, and for the same money we found we could go to the Continent and get a more thorough change.

At the gate, which H *half opens, they stand to say good-bye. It is a dark, stormy night, and as* C *shakes hands with his right hand he has to use all the strength of his left hand to prevent the heavy gate from being swung in against them.*

C: Good-bye, Mr. Hardy, and thank you so much—especially for going through those poems with me.

H: I must certainly do something about " The Interloper."

III

28 December 1920. *On returning to his hotel
after the last visit C finds that, when collecting the
papers which he had shown H, he has inadvertently
carried off the book of songs about which H had spoken
to him. On Wednesday morning he calls at Max Gate
to return the book. He is shown into the dining-room.*

*On one of the walls he notices a three-quarter-
length water-colour portrait of a woman whom he
takes to be the first Mrs. Hardy. The protrait is
that of a slim-figured, beautiful girl, in a blue and
white dress, with a long oval face, full features,
rich colouring, and brown ringlets (the " nut
brown " hair of the poems).*

Enter Mrs. H. *C returns the song book with
apologies.* Mrs. H *says it has not been required,
and that its absence had not been noticed.*

Mrs. H: I am sorry that Mr. Hardy is upstairs resting. But won't you stop a few minutes?

C: Thank you very much. . . . May I know
why the house is called Max Gate?

Mrs. H: You have noticed the little cottage
a few yards further up the road? It used to be a
toll-gate kept by a man called Mack. You will
remember that in the scene in *The Dynasts*, where
the beacon is lit on the Ridgeway, one of the
characters is made to say that from up there the

35

light at "Mack's Gate" can be seen. When my husband bought the plot of ground on which to build, Mack had been dead some time, but this point on the road was still known locally as Mack's Gate. My husband felt he could not call his house "Mack's Gate," but he wished to preserve the old association, and so he called it "Max Gate."

C: Yesterday I visited your husband's birthplace at Upper Bockhampton. Is the heath just beyond it a part of Egdon?

Mrs. H: Yes, that is Egdon Heath.

C: I think country like that looks more beautiful in winter than in summer.

Mrs. H: Yes, especially with the brown bracken. My husband thinks so too.

C: I was very lucky to have such a fine day after the gale of the night before. When I was here at Easter it was also extraordinarily mild. I remember your husband telling me of some flowers that were out unusually early. He dislikes cold weather very much, does he not?

Mrs. H: Yes, he says it freezes his brains.

C: I have noticed his dislike of it expressed very often in the poems. I suppose that the large majority of people do prefer summer to winter, and of course our language is full of the metaphorical use, in a forbidding sense, of words commonly applied to winter—"cold," "bleak," etc. But your husband's frequently expressed dislike of winter has struck me as almost strange in one who clearly has always been a great walker in all seasons and who shows such close observations of Nature in her inclement as well as her clement moods.

Mrs. H: I myself often feel very well in dry cold weather, but my husband says that it is very thoughtless to say " What a lovely frosty day " when one remembers all the suffering and cruelty it means to birds and other creatures.

C: The cottage was locked up. Is it inhabited?

Mrs. H: There is a tenant, but he is away at present. He is a Mr. Hermann Lea.

C: Oh, the author of *The Wessex of Thomas Hardy*. . . . Who is the owner?

Mrs. H: Mr. Hanbury.

C: Has Mr. Lea's lease got long to run?

Mrs. H: He hasn't it on a lease at all, but only on a quarterly tenancy.

C: I am sure that there are many people who would gladly contribute to a trust fund to buy it from Mr. Hanbury, so as to preserve it permanently for its literary interest.

Mrs. H: The whole of *Under the Greenwood Tree* and *A Pair of Blue Eyes*, and most of the *Return of the Native*, must have been written there.

C rises and says good-bye.

IV

The afternoon of 29*th December* 1920, *in the dining-room of Max Gate.*

Mrs. H: My husband has a headache and has been lying down. We went out to lunch, and though we drove there and back it was too much for him. I will go upstairs and see if he is well enough now to see you.

As she rises from her seat the door opens and H enters. C goes towards him and shakes hands.

H: Have you been far to-day?

C: Only to Lower Bockhampton and Staniford, to see the church. I had intended going along the Ridgeway, but it has been so wet to-day, and there would have been nothing to see on account of the mist.

H: On a clear day one gets a fine view of the sea from there.

C: I had a delightful walk yesterday. I went to Puddletown via Higher Bockhampton and the heath, crossed the road at Puddletown, and took a lane that led up on to Swaniston Hill. It made a very interesting round—of I suppose thirteen or fourteen miles.

H: As much as that? Yes, I dare say it would be.

C: I cut the ridge too near Dorchester to

pass the prototype of Bathsheba's house, but on my way to Puddletown I saw your birthplace.

Mrs. H [*going to the mantelpiece*]: You may be interested to see this model of the cottage. *She places on the table, between* C *and* H, *who is sitting opposite to him, a china replica, three or four inches in length.* C *examines it, and puts it down.* H *takes it up, and keeps it in his hands for some minutes, looking at it and turning it round. He points out to* C *that along the whole of the back of the cottage there is no window.*

H: I am told that owing to some structural difficulty it would not be possible to pierce any windows in the back wall.

C: You never made a drawing of the cottage?

H: No, but there is quite a nice photograph of it in Hermann Lea's book.

Mrs. H *hands the book to* C *open at the illustration.*

C: It does not show the rise of the ground above the house, which adds so much to the picturesqueness of its position.

H: No, that would be hard to get. . . . In my time the track at the back, leading up to the wood, was much lower than it is now. The ground is very steep there, and in the winter the rain pours down the slope carrying with it earth and rubbish which have raised the level considerably. When I was a boy and wanted to climb on to the roof for bird-nesting I had to use a long ladder. To-day one could almost reach with one's hand.

C: Did you ever think of making some drawings for any of the other volumes of verse, as you did for *Wessex Poems?*

H: No, it was too much labour. Besides, an artist can do it so much better.

C: There are some very pretty photographs in Hermann Lea's book.

H: Yes. He never intended to write a book at first, but after taking all the photographs he thought it was a pity not to put them to some use. I fear he has not made any money out of it. That is a pity. It discourages a man from going on writing.

C: His book is an invaluable mine of information about your books. I was amused to notice the variety of phrases he uses in identifying the various places: " we may claim it as the model," " there is ground for supposing that the author had in mind," " the city we think of as—" and so on. He is never satisfied to say merely " A is B."

H: That is the result of my coaching. I impressed on him that no place is taken exactly from an existing one.

C: Did you visit most of the places mentioned in *The Dynasts?*

H: A good many of them.

C: The descriptions of the towns are so vivid and the topography so thorough, that I felt sure you must have been over a great deal of the ground of the campaigns.

Mrs. H: Professor Oman told us that there were only about two points on which he was inclined to call in question my husband's accuracy, and that on going further into them he agreed that my husband was right.

H: Don't you think that it will be a long time before a truthful account of the Great War will be told?

C: I suppose so. I have read very many of the war books—Ludendorff, Von Tirpitz, Hindenburg, Czernin, Bethmann-Hollweg—but they do not seem to bring one any nearer the heart of things.

H: It is too soon. It will be a hundred years before the truth is known. Take the Napoleonic Wars. It was the conventional view for long that Napoleon never really intended to invade this country; that the camp at Boulogne was only a blind. Now, from documents that were revealed by Thiers, we know that he did intend to do so. ... Does Wells include the Great War in his History?

C: I have not read the book.

H: I think *Mr. Britling* is the best war book we have had. It gives just what we thought and felt at the time.

C: Have you met Wells?

H: Yes. He is a wonderfully energetic person. I see in the papers that he was going to America, but is ill and cannot go. I am not surprised.

C: Have you read any of D. H. Lawrence's books?

H: No. Does he write novels?

C: Novels and poetry.

Mrs. H: There is some of his poetry in the " Books of Georgian Verse."

H: Wasn't he a miner in Northumberland?

C: I don't think he himself was ever a miner. But his father was a miner in Nottinghamshire. He was a schoolmaster for some years. He has just published a new novel—*The Lost Girl*.

C: Mr. Hardy, if it is not asking too intimate a question, may I know whether there is any truth in the rumour that certain attacks in the press made on *Jude the Obscure* decided you not to write any more novels?

H [*shortly*]: Not just what the papers said. I never cared very much about writing novels. And I should not have—[*pause*]. Besides, I had written quite enough novels. Some people go on writing so many that they cannot remember their titles. There was a writer called Nat Gould—I forget how many he wrote.

C: I dare say one every six months. They were racing novels.

H: Yes, I have never read one of them.

42

C *gets up to leave. He first shakes hands with* Mrs. H *who is at the further left end of the fireplace, and then moves across the room to say goodbye to* H. *As he passes the bookshelf on the right of the fireplace he notices some editions of Thiers and other French historians.*

C [*to* H]: I suppose these are books you read for *The Dynasts?*

H: Yes. Some of them were very long and not very good. You may be sure I have not read them since.

C: I see you have the Pentland edition of Stevenson.

H: Why was it called the Pentland edition?

C: The Pentlands are a district in the Lowlands, are they not, by the Pentland Firth? Stevenson lived there at one time.

H: Somehow one cannot re-read Stevenson with much interest now. Don't you find it so?

C: I do. I was an immense admirer of him when I was young.

H: I doubt if he did any good to himself by going to Samoa. Don't you think he would have lived just as long if he had remained at Bournemouth? He was in this room once. He was passing through Dorchester. He had a mad scheme. He was going to Dartmoor, where he was to regain his health entirely. To Dartmoor—in October! He had a curious menagerie with him.

43

There was Louis; Mrs. Louis; a Mr. Strong; and a cousin.

C: Graham Balfour?

H: No, a woman: a pleasant, sensible Scotch girl. They went on to Exeter, and we heard nothing more of them for some time. I thought they were on Dartmoor, when one day I had a letter from Mrs. Louis from Exeter saying that Louis had been in a hotel there for months seriously ill. The Dartmoor plan was given up, and they returned to Bournemouth, to that house his father had bought for him—what was it called?

C: Skerryvore.

H: Yes.

C: There have been some interesting people in this room, Mr. Hardy.

H: Yes [*moving forward to open the door of the dining-room, and with the obvious intention of conducting C into the hall to say good-bye at the front door*].

C: Please do not trouble to come out into the cold, Mr. Hardy. Good-bye.

He shakes hands, and turns to leave the room. As he does so his eyes meet the portrait of the lady in the blue and white gown. Her gaze is directed straight in front of her—the full red lips half parted as if about to speak. The visitor forgets Stevenson, and Thiers, and Napoleon, and the war of a hundred years ago, and the Great War of

44

which the truth shall not be told for another hundred years. His thoughts go to the Poems of 1912-13: Veteris Vestigia Flammæ; *and to a grave in Mellstock Churchyard where that morning he had stood and watched the rain dripping on to a tomb-stone inscribed "Emma Lavinia Gifford—This for Remembrance," and to one who must have sat in that room for many hours during twenty years— one with whose influence, direct and indirect, on the life of her husband, there must be connected so much of the anguish and sadness, and the philosophy, and the beauty, of the works of Thomas Hardy.*

29 October 1921. 4.30 p.m. The drawing-room at Max Gate. Opposite the door leading from the hall is a door into the conservatory, which again faces a door into the garden. Enter C through the conservatory from the garden. He has already been received by Mrs. H. H is standing between the two doors looking out towards the garden. Mrs. H is sitting by the fire. C shakes hands with H.

C: I have been taking a photograph of the back of the house, but the light was not very good.

H: I fear you found the garden very messy after all the rain this morning.

C: The wind is drying it very quickly now. What fine chrysanthemums you have in the conservatory.

H: They have done well this year. They are all Mrs. Hardy's work. She planted them, watered them, staked them, potted them—everything.

C: They must have needed a lot of watering this dry summer, I am sure.

H: Won't you sit down? [*He points to a chair near the centre table, where tea is laid, which Mrs. H proceeds to serve. C sits down. H seats himself by the table on C's left, as on previous occasions.*]

C: I have a confession to make, Mr. Hardy,

46

of a theft, or rather two thefts. I have taken a cutting from the cotoneaster by the front door.

H: Cotoneasters are very easy to propagate. You can grow them quite easily from a berry.

C: Is not the cotoneaster in the front the bush you had in mind in that poem of yours about the snow—with your ingenious rhyme?

H: Yes. It has been there very many years.

Mrs. H: There's a seedling which has sowed itself just underneath the parent bush. If you like I will dig up that plant and send it to you.

C: Thank you very much.

H: They are wonderfully hardy. I have known a slip to strike when, in pruning, it has got lodged into the earth top-end in.

C: My other theft was over a year ago, when I first came here, and when I thought—I don't know if that mitigates or aggravates the crime —that I should only be seeing you for a few minutes and never again. I took a primrose plant from the drive.

H: Oh, a primrose.

C: I planted it in my garden, where it established itself so well that it survived a month of drought in the summer when I was away and there was no one to keep it watered. It has increased greatly, and a few days ago I divided it into about a dozen separate plants, and arranged them in a circle round a rose tree.

H: You have been luckier than I. When

47

I visited Scott's tomb at Dryburgh I found a wild strawberry growing near it, which I took. You know the wild strawberry? It is very small, but sweeter than the garden fruit. I planted it in the garden here, but forgot to tell the gardener. When some time after I looked for it, it was gone. He had dug it up and thrown it away. If it had been a primrose I suppose he would not have troubled to disturb it.

C: A gardener would have a special grudge against a wild strawberry just because it has a cultivated descendant.

The dog comes up to C *and rests his head on his knee.* H *orders him away.*

C: He does not bother me.

Mrs. H: Mr. Collins is not a postman!

C: I've heard how he dislikes the postman. [*Mrs. H has told* C *that the evening before he had bitten the postman, but that she hoped to keep her husband from knowing it.*] It is strange how dogs know visitors from tradesmen and others. I have a dog who will welcome any visitor who comes to the door or into the house, but will bark at a tradesman. They must recognize differences in clothes and walk. Have you noticed how even a good-tempered dog will bark at a beggar who is slouching along slowly?

H: Dogs are awful snobs. One can do a lot to ensure their respect by wearing a certain sort of glove.

48

C [*to* Mrs. H, *handing her a book which he has brought with him from London*]: I thought you would like to see this *Book of Women's Verse* by J. C. Squire, which the Oxford Press have just published.

Mrs. H: Thank you very much. I had heard of it.

H: Does he give any very early writers?

Mrs. H [*consulting the volume*]: He starts with Anne Askewe.

H: Dear me! I didn't know she had written poetry. [*To* C] Is it a good book?

C: The selection is very interesting, I think, but I am disappointed that in the introduction he does not deal more with the " feminine note in poetry "—I suppose there is one.

H: Certainly. One notices, for instance, how often women admire poems which men don't, and vice versa.

Mrs. H: I see he has not given anything by Miss Mew.

H: Nothing by Miss Mew! Perhaps he doesn't include any living writers.

Mrs. H: Yes, he has Frances Cornford and Mrs. Woods.

C: And Mrs. Meynell and others.

H: Miss Mew is far and away the best living woman poet—who will be read when others are forgotten.

C [*handing* H *a book*—Le Roman Anglais

de Notre Temps *by Abel Chevalley*]: My chief, Mr. Milford, who knew I was coming to see you, asked me to give you this book which he thinks may interest you. It shows a wonderful knowledge of the English novel in a Frenchman.

H: It is very kind of him. You will convey my thanks.

C: I am reading another book on English literature written in French—that study of your work by Mr. Hedgcock.

H: Oh yes. Mr. Hedgcock came here once.

C: His bibliography mentions a Hardy Dictionary by Saxelby. I thought of buying it. I suppose you know it.

H: I should not recommend you to buy it. It is merely a list of characters. I can't think why anyone should do such a book. He told me the idea was suggested to him by my having given the name of Saxelby to a character in one of my short stories.

C: Mr. Hedgcock also refers to Sherren's book, which I thought of buying.

H: It is merely a guide-book—not anything as good as Hermann Lea's.

C: Has anyone ever suggested a glossary of the dialect words which appear in your books?

H: No. There are not very many.

Mrs. H [*who had left the room and returns with a book*]: I see that Sir Henry Newbolt has given something of Miss Mew's in his anthology.

C: I was delighted to see what a large number of your poems he has included. There are nineteen.

H: I think he has made a good choice.

C: I suppose the English Association has arranged to include some of your poems in the second volume of *Poems of To-day*.

H: I am not sure.* Some of the anthologies that are published must be very successful. That book of modern verse published by Methuen has done surprisingly well. [Mrs. H *reaches a book from a shelf behind her and passes it to* C.]

C: I see it has been reprinted four times since May.

H: Do you think anthologies injure the sale of an author's books?

C: I should say that they tend to stimulate the sale.

H: I suppose so. I often get letters from people who have seen an extract from my work, telling me they are now starting to read me up.

Mrs. H: That was how I first got to know my husband's work.

H: From a book in a series called " Half Hours with Living Writers." I think afterwards it was called "Gleanings from Living Writers." In one of the volumes there was a selection from *A Pair of Blue Eyes*. They chose an extremely sensational passage—where Knight falls over the cliff.

* See footnote on page 6.

Mrs. H: I read it, and so was led on to read the whole novel. That is why I have been anxious to get a copy of the first edition. I secured one the other day. But it is not in the original binding, which I am told very much reduces its value.

H: I think it was a good bargain for thirty shillings.

Mrs. H: It was from the sale of Coventry Patmore's library by that second-hand bookseller—what is his name?

C: Everard Meynell?

Mrs. H: Yes.

H: Patmore liked that book best of all my novels. He said it ought to have been written in verse. So did Tennyson: " For my part I prefer *A Pair of Blue Eyes* to any of them." You know, Tennyson took to reading novels a lot in his later years.

C: I don't read novels as much now as I did when I was younger. I prefer poetry and biography.

H: So do I. Even the best novels I find it hard to read. I have never understood how Tennyson took that downward step.

C: Is the volume the Medici Society is publishing a reprint of your Golden Treasury selection?

H: Yes. I haven't seen the book yet.

C: Did you make that selection yourself?

H: I gave my approval to it. It represented

a consensus of opinion. I preferred to do it that way. It is very hard for an author to decide to make a selection from his own work. I found it very hard even with Barnes. It is easy enough to pick out the best and worst. The difficulty comes when one's space is limited and one has to chose from the large number of poems of intermediate value. . . . What a success the Golden Treasury Series has been. It has done a great deal to promote the reading of poetry.

C: I was glad to hear from Macmillan that when they reprint the *Collected Poems* they will add an index.

H: Won't that create a difficulty if later on fresh poems are put in?

C: It would involve alterations in the plates, or re-setting, but the cost would be negligible if spread over a fairly large edition.

Mrs. H: Would the volume stand being made much bigger?

H: Easily, if they used thinner paper. The Tennyson volume is a thousand pages or so.

C: Macmillan has promised to see if they can print a copy of the *Collected Poems* on India paper for me when they reprint.

Mrs. H [*pointing to Methuen's anthology*]: Is that India paper?

C: No, but it is very much thinner than what is used in the *Collected Poems*. It's a pretty volume.

H: I wish that when the *Oxford Dictionary*

is completed your people would consider the question of making the volumes more uniform in thickness, even if it involves spreading a letter over two volumes.

C: It would be very troublesome.

H: I went to Amen Corner once. I had written to ask when the Dictionary would be completed, and received rather an evasive reply. So when I was in London I called there. I dare say you were somewhere upstairs.

C: Is there any chance that the first novel you ever wrote will be published?

H: It no longer exists. When I was moving I got rid of it. It does not occur to authors when they are young that some day their early unsuccessful efforts may come to have value.

C: You may be interested to know that when I advertised a few days ago for a first edition of *Life's Little Ironies* I had five offers, varying from £2 10s. to 4s. 4d. I sent for the 4s. 4d. copy on approval, but it was a very shabby and dirty library copy. So I preferred to buy for the same price a good copy of the third impression. You remember *Life's Little Ironies* had three impressions in its first year.

H: I had forgotten that. You haven't a first edition of *Desperate Remedies?*

C: No.

H: There can't be many copies left. Only a small number were printed.

C: 750?

H: 500, I think.

C: Didn't some book-collector get hold of the letter you wrote to the publisher about it?

Mrs. H: Yes. [*She goes to a shelf, and produces Newton's book, which she hands to* C.]

H: He has printed a facsimile of the letter.

C [*finding the page*]: There it is.

H: He had no right to print a letter without leave. I suppose people count on authors not thinking it worth while applying for an injunction. However, I don't mind what they do with letters of mine they get hold of. They can only be business communications. [H *gets up from his chair and stands near* C *to read the facsimile.*] I paid Tinsley £75—I remember, in Bank of England £10 notes. He paid me back £60. So I lost £15 and all my labour. He was a shrewd chap when dealing with young authors. However, I always think that on a first novel a writer must not expect to make money. Old Tinsley must have sunk into poverty in his later years, for he asked me to help him to obtain a Civil List grant.

C: Used you to make many corrections in the MSS. of your novels?

H: It depended. If there was a passage of straightforward narrative there would not be many. There is no rule. . . . They tell us that Shakespeare never made any corrections. I

55

don't believe that. Ben Jonson, who said it, probably only saw a revised copy.

C: Did you prepare scenarios of the novels?

H: If I did I fear I did not follow them very closely. It was a hand-to-mouth matter—writing serials. I don't remember very well what I did. You see it is twenty-seven years since I wrote a novel. People write and ask me what I mean in a passage. Do they expect me to remember now what I meant over a quarter of a century ago?

C: Used you to have your novels typewritten? I believe publishers won't look at a novel now unless it is typed.

H: I had one or two.

C: To-day the typing and paper for a novel must be quite a considerable item of expense.

H: I notice the cost of paper myself, although I don't use much. There is some quarto paper we get. I used to buy so many sheets for 6s. 6d. It was in double sheets. Now I have to pay 9s.; and it is in single sheets—half as much.

C: Is there any chance of your bringing together some of your essays, etc., and making a volume of them?

H: It has been suggested. There is not very much.

C: I see Hedgcock refers to an essay you wrote on building a house.

H: That was a trifle—done for my pupils. A short time ago an American wrote a notice of me for some paper in which he said that I had published an article describing how I built Max Gate. My essay in *Chambers' Journal* was published twenty years before this house was built.

C: Has Macmillan ever suggested a selection of your poems for schools?

H: There is hardly need for that with the Golden Treasury selection. Great care was taken with it. It is quite fit for rectory drawing-rooms.

C: Are the Dorset Men going to do a dramatized version of one of your novels this year?

H: No. At the present moment interest is monopolized by the musical society here, which is going to perform some of the Gilbert and Sullivan operas. Of course it is comparatively easy to make a success of them. They have been done thousands of times. It is very different with an entirely new play. The dramatic society engaged the hall for a particular date, and the musical society went one better by engaging it for a month earlier.

Mrs. H: There have been other obstacles too. Tilley is not able to give any time, as his father is ill, and he has to devote all his leisure to being with him. Then Miss Bugler has married, and lives outside Dorchester.

C: What novel had they proposed to do?

H: *Desperate Remedies.* And a very melodramatic version they have made. I asked Barrie whether he thought it mattered letting them

57

treat my books in that way. He said he would leave them to do just what they like.

C *looks at his watch.*

H: Where are you stopping?

C: I am returning to London to-night by the 7 o'clock train.

Mrs. H: Won't that be very tiring? I have done it once or twice, and been exhausted.

H: One ought not to be really. If one takes things easily a day or two beforehand it makes a lot of difference. The Masefields were here the other day: they left London in the morning; stopped here very late; and went on in the evening to Galsworthy on Dartmoor.

Mrs. H [*to* H]: You remember how tired your sister Mary used to be.

H: She used to go up to London in the morning, visit the Royal Academy, and return in the evening. She did not like sleeping in London, but she loved to see the pictures.

Mrs. H [*to* H]: The last time she did this she nearly collapsed at the station when she got back. But then she was over seventy. [*To* C] However, if you think so little of coming down here and going back the same day it makes me feel I really ought to go up. I should enjoy a week in London very much.

H: I should too—when once I was there. But perhaps it is hardly worth while.

Mrs. H: What is the present condition of

58

the publishing trade? There was a bad time in the spring, I was told, but I understand it is better now.

C: My own work is chiefly with educational books. The sale of these is very fair. But production is still very dear.

H: I suppose high wages are the cause?

C: Yes. There's a movement towards reduction of wages.

H: It seems very short-sighted of the wage-earners not to realise that some things are not necessities. Each trade thinks that what it does is necessary. Take gardening. One generally has some cutting of trees done now. But one says to oneself " A man will cost so much. I will let the garden go this year." Or you do it yourself.

C: Mr. Hardy, I know you must be often bothered for autographs, but I should be very grateful if you would put your name to this copy of the first edition of *Satires of Circumstance.* Would you write it on the half-title of " Poems of 1912-13," which is the section I love most of all your work? [C *hands him the book open at that part of the volume.*]

H: I had better write at the beginning of the book.

C: My own name is already written there. [*He offers* H *a fountain pen.*]

H: There are really two poems in another

part of the volume which belong to that sequence.

C: I know. You have added them to it in the *Collected Poems*.

H [*turning over the pages, and pointing to " St. Launce's Revisited "*]: That is one. Where is the other? It's called " Where the Picnic was." Ah, there it is.... I think I had better sign where I generally do. [*He turns back to the general half-title, and underneath " Satires of Circumstance " writes " Thomas Hardy." The writing is clear and steady.*]

C: Thank you very much. I fear it's a very bad nib. Do you use a fountain-pen?

H: I press so heavily on my pen that I should ruin one. I suppose they hold quite a lot of ink? It does not dry up?

C: I should think there's enough ink in this to write about twenty quarto sheets.

H: Really!

C *rises to go.* H *and* Mrs. H *get up.*

Mrs. H: On the table by the clock there's a medallion of my husband. [C *goes to the side-table, and takes the medallion to the centre table to examine it under the light of the lamp. It gives* H's *left profile.*] I'm told it is a better likeness if one looks at it from the right. It is considered very good.

C: I think it is. The nose, though, is not quite right—too much of the conventional Duke of Wellington Roman nose.

Mrs. H: Yes.

C: Can copies be bought?

Mrs. H: I think so. I will give you the sculptor's address. [*She goes to her desk and returns with a notebook in which she points out an address —Spicer Simpson, 57 West 57 Street, New York City. C writes it down.*]

H: You had better put " Hardy Medallion " or you will forget what it is about.

C *returns the medallion to the side-table. In doing this he notices, on another table, a wooden model of a full-rigged sailing ship, about three feet long. He stops to look at it. On the deck is written " From J. Masefield, poet, to Thomas Hardy, poet, with homage."*

H: That was given to me by Masefield. He brought it down here the other day.

C: It is very nicely done.

H: I told him I didn't know why he had spent so much trouble making it for me, but he said he enjoyed doing it. You know he was a sailor. I think *Dauber* is his best book.

C: Didn't Strang do a portrait of you which has recently been engraved?

H: Yes, he did two: one just before his death.

C: I heard about it in the spring, from a friend of his, a Dr. Thursfield.

H: He had a great reputation. I don't know if I cared very much for his work.

C: May I, before I go, read the inscription

61

on a photograph of Galsworthy which I think hangs on the left of the fireplace?

Mrs. H: It is now on the book-case on the left of the fire, behind that picture of Nicholsons'.

C [*goes across the room to the book-case. The picture is a photogravure of " The Girl with the Tattered Glove," with an autograph inscription to H by the artist. C takes it in his hand and turns towards the lamp on the centre table.*] It's a beautiful thing.

H [*who has followed C, and is standing on his left*]: Yes, there's something very attractive about it—one can't say exactly what.

C: Do you know where the original is?

H: In the FitzWilliam at Cambridge, I think. I suppose that picture has made Nicholson more famous than anything else.

C *takes up the framed photograph of Galsworthy and places it on the table.*

C: How long ago was it taken?

Mrs. H: About ten years ago, I should think.

The inscription is: " *The optimist appears to be one who cannot bear the world as it is, and is forced by his nature to picture it as it ought to be; and the pessimist one who can not only bear the world as it is, but loves it well enough to draw it faithfully.*"
—The Inn of Tranquillity.

H *reads it at the same time as* C.

H: " Inn of Tranquillity "—is that the name of one of his books?

C: Yes, containing a story of that title.

H: I shouldn't say " loves." He need not necessarily love it. It may be because he is indifferent enough.

Mrs. H: Yes.

H: Why are people always talking about " pessimism "? In the past a poet was not labelled in that way. He was allowed to write as he thought and felt. The other day we had an Eton master here. He talked about pessimism and pessimists. I pointed to Gray. You know his poem on Eton? What could be more " pessimistic "?

C: " Alas, regardless of their doom
    The little victims play!
No sense have they of ills to come,
    Nor care beyond to-day:
Yet see how all around them wait
The Ministers of human fate,
    And black Misfortune's baleful train!"

H: And still stronger further on: " Grimvisag'd comfortless Despair "; "Moody Madness laughing wild amid severest woe "; and so on. . . . " Oh, Gray is an unbearable poet " was his remark. That's how they get out of it. I suppose "pessimism" is an easy word to say and remember. It's only a passing fashion.

H, Mrs. H, *and* C *go into the hall, where* H

lights a lantern. Mrs. H, *with a lamp, leads* C *upstairs to show him* H's *study. It is a medium-sized, square room. All four walls are lined with bookshelves. In the middle of the room is a desk, and a plain mahogany straight-backed chair with leather seat. Near the desk is a small low table, and drawn up to this table is a low chair with curved back, upholstered in cretonne. Against the shelves on the left of the door as one enters is a narrow sofa, also upholstered in cretonne.*

Mrs. H: This is the room where he has written nearly all his work. It has hardly ever been changed. [*Catching* C's *glance*] That sofa has been there the whole time.

C: Has he always used that chair to write in?

Mrs. H: He tried another, but did not like it.

C *descends into the hall with* Mrs. H, *to whom he says good-bye.*

C *thanks* H *for letting him see his study.* H, *without hat or coat, accompanies* C *along the drive,* C *holding the lantern. At the gate he gives the lantern to* H *and says good-bye.*

V I

19 *August* 1922. *Scene as at the last interview.
Present,* Mrs. H *and* C. Mrs. H *is showing* C
*some drawings and a fan presented to her husband
the day before by a Japanese professor, when* H
enters, as if not expecting to find a visitor.

H: Oh—Mr. Collins! . . . I am very glad to
see you.

C: Mrs. Hardy has been showing me this
Japanese fan. . . . She tells me that *Tess* has been
translated into Japanese.

H: *Tess of the D'Urbervilles?* Yes.

C: But only half of it, I hear. That is
strange.

Mrs. H: The professor from Tokio explained
that the latter portion of the book would not
appeal to the Japanese. It would be outside
their comprehension. In Japan it is thought a
virtuous thing for a girl to sell herself to obtain
money for the help of her family. There would
not seem to them to be any tragedy in Tess
living with Alec d'Urberville.

H: The whole book would be rather long for
the Japanese. They like literary works to be
very short. They realize that short poems live
the longer.

C: What about the great epics?

H: Even of them it is only passages that are remembered.

C: Chaucer?

H: Chaucer too. Shakespeare's songs are the best known and most commonly repeated parts of his plays. Or take Ben Jonson—" Drink to me only with thine eyes."

C [*to Mrs.* H]: I hope you did not write in reply to my last letter to say that you and your husband would have liked to see that volume of Blake's drawings? I had to alter my plans and leave town last night, and I've been fearing that a letter might be lying at my office this morning asking me to bring the book down.

Mrs. H: We decided that we were not sufficiently interested in his drawings to trouble you to bring such a big volume all this way. I think I admire Blake more than my husband does —in fact, I'm sure I do. My husband is always a little repelled by the evident streak of insanity in him. But at his best he is a glorious genius.

H: Twenty or thirty years ago, when Blake was not known as well as he is now, I remember Macmillan's showing me some of his drawings. They were originals and very remarkable. I don't know what happened to them—whether they were published. There was one extraordinarily fine one, of Moses.

C: The particular drawings I wrote about were only discovered recently—in the library

66

of the Duke of Hamilton. They consist of illustrations to Gray's Poems of 1768, and were done by Blake as a present to Mrs. Flaxman.

H: Blake is a poet who benefits by selections —like Wordsworth. Many people buy a volume of Wordsworth, happen to read some of his worst poetry, and imagine it's his best.

C: What a pity it is that so many poets apparently allow everything they write to be published.

H: An author cannot always tell what people will like most. Posterity alone can decide. So I generally publish everything. When I have been in doubt (as I was, for example, with my last volume) about two or three poems, I afterwards found that those were often what some people liked best; and poems I have been on the point of discarding have sometimes been used in anthologies. . . . What a number of anthologies there are now!

C: Since I saw you last the question has been discussed in the *Times Literary Supplement* whether a poet is benefited or injured by the inclusion of his poems in anthologies.

H: Yes, I saw that. What do you think?

C: Unless a poet enjoys extremely wide popularity like, say, Kipling, I think it's to his advantage.

H: I think so too. . . . Did I ever tell you the story of a man who wrote to me some years ago, before Macmillan told me I ought to charge, asking leave to include some poems in an anthology? He said that if I would tell him my terms he would tell me his publisher. I had never thought of charging him anything. I did not care for this way of doing business and did not answer his letter. He next wrote to say that some of my poems were not copyright. (Now and then I intentionally gave out that some of my poems were free, when I was anxious for them to be reprinted and known.)

C: Such as " Men who march away "?

H: Yes. . . . Well, I replied at once telling him by all means to use those. Three months afterwards I read in the papers that he was in gaol for getting money under false pretences.

C: Which of the younger English poets of to-day do you think the best?

H: It's very hard to say. One is often affected by one's personal liking for the writer. I like Blunden very much. He's been down here. You know he's quite a boy—a sort of Shelley, and he does the sort of things Shelley would have done.

C: Have you read Lascelles Abercrombie's last book of plays?

H: No, I saw it had been published. He is better as a critic than a poet. Some of his poems are much too long.

C: And obscure too—but these plays are

68

quite simple. I liked them very much. . . . [*To* Mrs. H*] You saw that Hudson is dead?

Mrs. H: Yes.

H: I am very sorry.

C: He came into his fame very late.

H: Yes, and very suddenly.

C: But in the end he had very high recognition, though of course he was never popular. I think the best judges considered his work the finest English prose written in recent years.

H: I dare say it was. I don't know his books as well as I should like.

C: They must have sold pretty well in recent years. You know he gave up his Civil List pension?

Mrs. H: That was very good of him—though one would have liked to think of his benefiting from it to get some luxuries in his old age. But perhaps he was not a man of that sort.

C: Probably not. I know someone who saw him a few weeks ago—Mrs. Thomas, widow of Edward Thomas. She had never met him before, but he had known her husband well, and was writing a preface for a volume of sketches he had left. Hudson said to her in parting " Will you let an old man, who has more money than he needs for himself, say that if ever I can be of help to you I hope you will let me know?"

H: That was very generous. Did he live in Cornwall?

C: I think he lived in London a part of the year.

H: He must have lived in Cornwall at one time. He wrote a book about it—*Land's End*. He must have travelled a lot when he was young.

C: When in London he used to lunch at Whiteley's every day, Mrs. Thomas told me.

Mrs. H: How very different from what one would have thought he would do.

H: Even Harrod's would have been better. When we were in London we lived near Whiteley's and used to lunch there sometimes, but more often at Harrod's just because it was further away.

Mrs. H: How old was he?

C: The notice in the *Daily Chronicle* says " somewhat over 80." Mrs. Thomas thought he looked about 65—thin, but erect and full of fire.

H: Had he been ailing long?

C: He told her that he was very ill.

H: He must have been a very reserved man. In *Who's Who* he gives very few particulars of himself—not even his age. It must have been very sad for him to outlive all his friends. I have lost several people lately. A friend of mine in Yorkshire died suddenly the other day. I had no idea he was even ill. And Miss Genevieve Ward. It's many years since I saw her.

C: And Raleigh.

H: Yes, of course: I knew there was some-one I was omitting. The last time I saw him was when I stopped with him at Oxford at the time of the performance of *The Dynasts*. He looked very ill then. I noticed how his hands trembled. What a strange thing it was for him to take up that book on the War in the Air, and to go in for flying himself. Whatever made him do it? It was too different from what he was used to.

C: He was always rather fond of by-paths.

H: People dissipate their efforts in under-takings like this. It is often worse than doing nothing. . . .

Mrs. H: I am sorry about Mr. Hedgcock's book.*

C: Pray say no more about it. I was of course disappointed, but when I realized that you were not favourably disposed to the idea I should not have taken any satisfaction in going on even if Mr. Hedgcock had not independently decided that he could not make all the alterations you desiderated and that he preferred to abandon the proposal.

H: When the book appeared in French I did

* A short time before this interview a project for an English translation to be done by me of Mr. F. A. Hedgcock's *Thomas Hardy: Penseur et Artiste* (Hachette, 1913) had been abandoned when Thomas Hardy raised objections to the biographical part of the book.—V.H.C.

71

not think it worth while to take seriously the things I objected to, as I understood it to be only a thesis connected with Mr. Hedgcock's Paris degree.

C: My own general view was that it was a thorough and interesting piece of work, and, after Lionel Johnson's and Lascelles Abercrombie's books, far better than anything else I have read on your novels, though I do not agree with all the opinions expressed: for example, in the depreciation of *Tess of the D'Urbervilles* and *Jude the Obscure;* nor are Mr. Hedgcock and I at one about your poetry.

H: As the book is ten years old it is of course out of proportion, for I have now written verse for twenty-seven years and prose only twenty-five.

C: A chapter on your later verse was to have been added, and I think another chapter would have been required for *The Dynasts.*

H: What would have been done with the long extracts from the novels?

C: Some of them would have been abridged or omitted.

H: I have no objection to legitimate literary criticism of my works, favourable or otherwise, but Mr. Hedgcock is continually drawing on the novels for description of my character. His dissection would not be in good taste while I am still alive, even if it were true. But it is based chiefly on characters and incidents in the novels that are pure invention. I should have imagined that he would not like at this date to have personal quizzing of that immature sort revived as his work.

C: I had hoped that the references you object to could be altered. When you wrote to me about them I told Mr. Hedgcock, but presumably he was unwilling to carry out all the alterations you desired.

H: Errors of that sort are long-lived and are repeated by others. Some of them appear in Professor Chew's book.

C: I don't know that book.

H: It's published in America. I will get it and show it to you. [*He leaves the room and returns with Professor Chew's and Mr. Hedgcock's books.*]

C [*looking at the former*]: I must buy a copy.

H: You had better wait until a new edition is published. I can't lend you this copy, as it is marked, and Professor Chew, who is coming here again, will want to borrow it. . . . [*Opening Mr. Hedgcock's book*] Why are people not more careful in deducing biographical and semi-biographical facts from an author's books? People used to say that David Copperfield was Dickens. He was not. [*He turns over the pages of the book*] Mr. Hedgcock's besetting fault of getting behind the novels of the writer leads to numerous inaccuracies. Thus he says that I

73

was brought up to speak the local dialect. I did not speak it. I knew it, but it was not spoken at home. My mother only used it when speaking to the cottagers, and my father when speaking to his workmen. The account of my education is full of errors. It is stated that I was educated at an elementary school and was deprived of a classical training. I was only at an elementary school for a year or two, till I was ten, and I learnt Latin at school from my twelfth year. Again, he says I learnt the classics by correspondence—deluded by his false identification of me with Smith in *A Pair of Blue Eyes*. The same source of error leads to the ascription to myself of the disgust felt for architecture by a character in *Desperate Remedies*. At other times in his desire to give biographical details he simply invents. He gives the impression that I lived all my life in Dorset, except short absences now and then to the Continent and elsewhere. For about thirty years I spent three or four months every year in London. All the false deductions in this chapter would be impertinent and unmannerly about a living writer even if they were not false. When he comes to Smith he makes some of his worst mistakes—one unwarranted assumption after another. The description of his appearance is not at all like what I was. His father was not at all like mine. He was a Cornish man and a journeyman. Smith himself was a

74

Weymouth man—as far as he was based on any real person, which he was not much. On one page he identifies me with Springrove, and on another with Clym.... I cannot understand how he could print such stuff.... I wish I could show you a photograph of the person Smith was based on. I should not have been so conceited as to make myself the prototype. I describe him as a tall, handsome young fellow. He was a fellow-pupil of mine when I was in an architect's office. He must be seventy years old now. He does not know he appears in the book.

C: Isn't he a reader?

H: No. He got on very well in his profession, and held a big post under the Government in the war.

C: Was he only a prototype of Smith physically?

H: The adventures ascribed to Smith did not happen to him. But he was the sort of person to whom such adventures might have happened. It is easy for an author to take a person, and see the potentialities in his temperament for the events he creates.

C: You might be interested to know of an event happening in my own experience—in my own family—which reminds one very much of the theme in one of *Life's Little Ironies*, " On the Western Circuit," though not followed by such tragic results. When I was a boy my maternal grandmother and grandfather who lived in Canada used often to come over for a trip to Europe with an aunt of mine—at that time unmarried. A girl friend of this aunt and of the family—a very pretty and considerably younger girl than my aunt—who had recently been left an orphan, was on one occasion invited by my grandparents to accompany them to Europe. They went to Aix-les-Bains, and there, in the Casino, this girl, Miss B——, got to know a young officer in the Italian army. They fell in love with one another, and became informally engaged. As neither could speak the other's language or more than a few words in French, I don't know how they succeeded in conversing. Perhaps, as I think you have put it in one of your stories, " lips and eyes helped out what tongue could not express."

H: I don't remember writing that—but it's very good.

C: On various occasions my aunt, who knew Italian well, acted as interpreter. She also had secretly fallen in love with the young man. When my grandparents left Aix-les-Bains to return to Canada the correspondence between the young couple was carried on by my aunt, who had to read and translate into English for Miss B—— the letters that came from Italy, and to translate and write in Italian the letters Miss B—— dictated. Eventually Miss B——, who was a bit of a flirt, and was ambitious to make a good match, decided to break off the engagement with a penniless officer, and to marry another suitor who was better off. It devolved on my aunt to convey this news to the young Italian. Her letters were expressed with such sympathy that a correspondence continued between him and her. A year or two later my aunt paid another visit to Europe with her parents, met him again, became engaged to him, and eventually married him—I am glad to say, most happily.

H: It's certainly most remarkably similar.

Mrs. H: That is my favourite story in *Life's Little Ironies*.

C: Mine too. On several occasions when I have been asked to read to persons who do not know your husband's work I have selected that.

Mrs. H: When we were in London some time ago, stopping with Mr. Justice Darling, we went into his court one day at the Bailey. The case that was being tried was of some young scoundrels who had been had up for piracy. It was obvious that the defending barrister knew he had a hopeless task. He was a young man of about thirty—very handsome (you know how a wig enhances the effect of a well-cut profile); one could see he was a dreamer. There to the very life was Charles Ray.

H: When I had written the story I gave it to Sir Francis Jeune to read for fear I had gone wrong in the legal details. Jeune returned the MS. to me and said that the only mistake I had made was in saying that Ray's absence at the next assize town was not noticed. (You remember he remained behind.) Jeune said that it would have been noticed, but that I could make it all right by saying that he had to stop on for an arbitration case. That's why I put this in. Some years later I told another judge—Cave, I think—about it, and said how glad I was I had not fallen into a pitfall. I read him out the passage. He said that the introduction of the arbitration case was quite unnecessary: no one would have noticed his absence.

Mrs. H: So judges disagree as well as doctors.

H [*to* Mrs. H]: Doctors—yes! [*Taking up Mr. Hedgcock's book*] Would you like to take this away with you? I have marked in the margins the errors in the biographical chapter. I have not re-read all the rest of the book. You might like to go through my annotations at your leisure.

C: Thank you very much. May I show them to Mr. Hedgcock?

H: Certainly. I should be quite glad to see a translation published if he would make the alterations I have indicated.

C: How do you like Blanche's portraits, which are reproduced in it? Mr. Hedgcock told me that you had refused to accept the original of one of them.

78

H: It was never offered to me. But perhaps now I think of it, what I said would have given the impression that I did not care for it. The finished portrait is a much better one than the study. [*Opening the book at the latter*] Now can you see me in that? It was done fifteen years ago, and it makes me look about ninety.

Mrs. H: It's very much nicer in the original.

C: Where is the original?

Mrs. H: In the Tate Gallery. It was presented by Mr. Debenham.

C: Is the finished portrait there too?

H: I think Mr. Debenham must have that in his house. He bought both.

C: Is Blanche well known?

H: He has been called the French Sargent. In his later years he got impoverished, and he was sold up. I was very sorry. But I did not know the way to treat him. When I was in Paris he was painting another portrait, of a Mrs. ——, a very pretty woman. She criticized something in the protrait, and Blanche at once drew his brush across it. Mrs. —— burst into tears: " Oh, you've destroyed my pretty portrait." Afterwards I saw another he did of her—a magnificent picture. When I was sitting I passed no criticisms. If I had, he would have done another and better portrait of me.

Mrs. H: Talking of portraits, what do you think of this? [*She shows* C *a water-colour por-*

trait (about twelve inches . by ten).] Do you think it is a practical joke?

C: I certainly don't see any likeness to your husband, nor any beauty in line or colour. But I am not a judge of painting. Who did it?

Mrs. H: It's supposed to be by A——. There's a young man called B—— who wanted to paint my husband. He presented me with this when he came here to arrange for a sitting —imagining that I am all-powerful in this house to make my husband do what I want—which I am not.

H: Which you are.

Mrs. H: I'm told that even the drawing is bad, and it does not look as if it was finished.

C: If it was done by A—— I should think it must have been a ten-minutes' study which he threw away, and which B—— picked up. . . . When will the new edition of Lionel Johnson's book about you be ready?

H: I don't know. I thought it was foolish to reprint it. It was written so many years ago.

C: Before even *Jude the Obscure.*

H: Yes. Lane is having a chapter added on my poetry. But that is out of proportion. I have now been writing poetry more years than I wrote prose. However, Lane said that if he did not do it someone else would. He told me he had already sold a thousand copies of the new edition.

C: I know there is a considerable demand for the original book. When I bought it a few years ago I think I paid 25s. . . . What will happen to your *Collected Poems* now that *Late Lyrics and Earlier* has been published?

H: I shall have it added at the end of the volume when there is a reprint.

C: It will be all the more desirable to have a thin-paper edition then.

H: Yes, I have seen to that. . . .

C [*to* Mrs. H]: I've arranged to stay over the night with some friends at Swanage. Have you a local time-table you can let me see?

Mrs. H [*going to a desk and producing a time-table, which she consults*]: There's a train to Swanage at seven. You could just do it if you knew the short cut across the fields. [*To* H] Would you care to show Mr. Collins the way?

H: Certainly. You are coming too? [Mrs. H *assents*.] I'll wrap up Mr. Hedgcock's book for you. [*He leaves the room.*]

C: Your husband is looking very well.

Mrs. H: Yes. He was seriously ill in the winter.

C: I am sorry to hear that. I had not known.

Mrs. H: The doctors suspected all sorts of terrible things, but he ended by getting well simply by staying in bed. He is much better now, though as a matter of fact he stopped in bed until twelve to-day—a very unusual thing with him: he is nearly always up by nine, and anxious to start the day's work.

C: He certainly seemed very bright to-day.

Mrs. H: You can't always go by that. Seeing people stimulates him.

Mrs. H *and* C *go into the hall.* H *is standing just inside the dining-room, which opens into the hall opposite to the drawing-room.*

H: Here is Mr. Hedgcock's book. [*He holds a brown-paper parcel in his hand.* C *steps inside the dining-room to take it from him.* H *turns round and moving towards the further end of the room points to the portrait of himself over the sideboard.*] Now that seems to me a good piece of work. But perhaps in years to come people will not like that style of painting.

H *and* C *rejoin* Mrs. H *in the hall. All three leave the house, walk down the drive and out through the gate, and crossing the road go along a footpath across some fields.* H *walks briskly.*

H [*pointing to a field on the left*]: They have nearly got in all the corn to-day, and are working overtime. They ought to work on Sunday to finish. Before the repeal of the Corn Laws they used always to work on Sundays at harvest time. It will be raining within twenty-four hours. Look at the clouds over the Monument.*

C: What has happened about the cottage?

* The Monument of Captain Hardy, Nelson's captain.

Mrs. H: Hermann Lea has left, and there's another tenant—the Secretary of the Dorset Field Club. He is not living there himself, but has put two of his sons in, who are engaged in chicken and duck farming.

C: Has the cottage been repaired?

H: It has been thatched. In the old days thatching was done with freshly cut corn. The heads were cut off, and the reeds were used as they were. In that condition they were very straight and strong. But now on account of shortage the corn has to be threshed first, and so one gets only straw, which is not so strong.

C: Had you contemplated a book on the Napoleonic Wars long before you actually started writing *The Dynasts?*

H: I had long been interested in Napoleon. I should think I started making notes about 1880. I collected a lot of material, and then thought it a pity not to make use of it.

C: Were you ever in Russia?

H: No.

C: The other day I was reading Fisher's little book on Napoleon in the 'Home University Library.' He says that Napoleon never tried to commit suicide.

H: It's a very controversial point. He may have done it in a semi-serious way for effect. Anyhow, there's enough evidence to justify the introduction of the incident into an imaginative work.

C: Have you read Trench's *Napoleon?*

H: That's the play where Napoleon is supposed to come to England? No. There's something strange there. I wrote a story called " A Tradition of Eighteen Hundred and Four." I had a long discussion with Colvin about the place where he might have landed. We were agreed that it could only be Lulworth Cove. I mentioned that it was a tradition in order to add credibility to the tale. There was not any tradition. I invented it.

C: I will send you a copy of Trench's book if I may.

H: I should be very much obliged if you would lend it to me. I won't say if I will keep it until I have read it.

C: Will you ever write any memoirs of your life?

H: No. I won't compete with Mrs. Asquith and Lloyd George. Several American professors have urged me to write them. They come to see me from all parts of America. I had one all the way from Tennessee. They ask all sorts of questions about one's private life.

On coming to a railway bridge H *directs* C *how to find his way by a path along the line, across some sidings, and into the station—about ten minutes' walk.* C *shakes hands with* Mrs. H *and then with* H.

C: Thank you so much for everything, and

especially, if it is not invidious to discriminate, for this delightful and unexpected walk.

They part. H *and* Mrs. H *turn in their home-ward direction. When a few yards off* C *looks back to catch a last sight of them. They have reached the middle of the bridge.* C *sees them stop. They remain standing there, facing towards the station.**

---

* Extract from a letter to me from Mrs. Hardy a few days later: "You did not know that my husband insisted on waiting at the bridge until your train had passed. If you had known you could not have seen us, and he knew that we should not see you. It was a curious act of sentiment on his part—I suppose the same feeling which prompts some people to wait to see a ship out of sight when it has borne a friend away."—V.H.C.